In Dedication: *Written and dedicated to Julie Gervasi My wife, partner in ministry, and help. You have always complimented me and make me a better person.*

Library of Congress Control Number: 2025920698

The Going Deeper
Study Guide–Group Edition
Part 1

Pastor Frank & Samuel Gervasi

MIDWEST CHRISTIAN PUBLISHING

ISBN: 979-8-9993044-7-6

Introduction:

Whether you are someone who has a good walk with the Lord or just wanting to draw closer to Christ. Every person of faith finds themselves wanting or needing of a better connection with God. For the person who has drifted, we don't always remember how it happened or how we arrived at that point in our spiritual journey. However, we are all at one time or another, awakened by the realization that we want more of God.

We remember as David did in the Psalms, times where we enjoyed our relationship and our closeness with God. He says, *"These things I remember as I pour out my soul: how I used to go to the house of God under the protection of the Mighty One with shouts of joy and praise among the festive throng." (Psalm 42:4, NIV)* So, we make the decision and commitment to grow in our faith and press hard after God once again. All to experience the thriving faith that we want for ourselves.

Our hope and prayer are that you take these next fifteen to thirty lessons with the *Going Deeper Study Guide-Group Edition* and be purposeful in pressing hard after God through these *Interactive Lessons*. They were edited for a Group/Teaching Format. However, they can be used for individual study also. Each day has a *Memory* Verse & passages that will help the reader be reminded of God's Faithfulness and Goodness. The *Big Idea* for that *Lesson* and passage giving the main point or permanent principle, *Scripture Assignments,* and an *expanded* take-away thought in the *Insight* section with *Application* portion. Along with a *Weekly Challenge* and *Prayer* sections to solidify the *Lesson* and growth for that respective *Topic.* Additionally, each *Lesson* includes a *Going Deeper* section that features some writer, commentator, or expanded reference for the day's passage or ideas, along with a *Going Deeper Response Section*.

We hope you faithfully use and enjoy the *Going Deeper Study Guide.*

Going Deeper
Study Guide
Group Edition

Part 1

by Pastor Frank & Samuel Gervasi

Table of Contents:

Lesson 1 - Crowning of the King

Memory Verse: *"I tell you, He replied. 'If they keep quiet the stones will cry out.'"* **Luke 19:40, NIV**

Open in Prayer:

Introduction

Every day, when the sun rises over Washington, D.C., it's light first falls on the eastern side of the city's tallest structure, the 555-foot Washington Monument. The first part of this historic monument is to reflect the rising Sun on the eastern side of its aluminum capstone, where one will see the Latin words inscribed, *Laus Deo,* which when translated into English reads, *"Praise be to God."*

Praise is one of the most discussed topics in scripture. In fact, our reading today probably shows one of the greatest moments of worship that Christ experiences on this side of heaven. In our passage, we see the people exalt Christ as King as He rides triumphantly into Jerusalem and give Him the worship He's due. *1*

Read: *Luke 19:35-40*

"They brought it to Jesus, threw their cloaks on the colt and put Jesus on it. 36 As he went along, people spread their cloaks on the road. 37 When he came near the place where the road goes down the Mount of Olives, the whole crowd of disciples began joyfully to praise God in loud voices for all the miracles they had seen: 38 'Blessed is the king who comes in the name of the Lord!' 'Peace in heaven and glory in the highest!' 39 Some of the Pharisees in the crowd said to Jesus, 'Teacher, rebuke your disciples!" 40 "I tell you,' he replied, 'if they keep quiet, the stones will cry out.'" (NIV)

John MacArthur calls this passage, *"the Coronation of the King,"* **2** and references it as Christ's last public appearance before His crucifixion. Which I think is an appropriate title for this passage, because it sounds more regal, like a ceremony for royalty. And this was in part, exactly the reason the people of Jerusalem are worshipping with such joy.

1. **What Other Reasons Could the Crowd Have Been Excited to Worship Jesus?**

   a._____

   b._____

   c._____

   d._____

In v. 37 it says, *"When he came near the place where the road goes down the Mount of Olives, the whole crowd of disciples began joyfully to praise God in loud voices for all the miracles they had seen."* It was finally time!

2. **What Barriers Stand in the Way of Keeping a Reverence for the Things of God?**

   a.   _____

   b.   _____

   c.   _____

Consider how they had been hearing about the coming Messiah for so many years throughout the Old Testament readings in the various synagogues. Week after week! Year after year! Reading after reading! They had realized something important: that Jesus was the only true King, worthy of our worship and obedience. And we too need to understand this because how we view Christ and worshipping Him can make a difference.

3. **What Do the Following Verses Say About Worship:**

Psalm 22:29	
Psalm 29:2	
Psalm 55:14	
Psalm 81:9	

4. How Can Submission Be Related to Reverence? *(Explain your Answer)*

_____

_____

_____

_____

5. What Areas Do I Need to Submit to God in a Greater Way? *(Explain Your Answers)*

a_____

b_____

c_____

d_____

See, the crowd understood that this was a big deal for these people and the time had arrived. They worship Him with their whole heart!

Insight: Christ Being King Should Mean that a Person Worships Christ in Reverence. However, it Also Means That After We Submit Our Life to Him, -That We Live in Ways That Are Consistent With His Teachings

6. What Do the Following Verses Show About Submission?

Romans 13:1	
1 Cor. 14:34	
Hebrews 5:7	

What is my general mindset towards praise?

_____

_____

_____

Is it like in the passage? Yes or No (Circle One) (Explain Your Answer)

_____

_____

How can I improve my outlook on praise? _____

_____

_____

Going Deeper:

In this passage, you may notice that Jesus comes into Jerusalem on what some Gospels describe as a *"donkey."* However, Matthew includes the word *foal"* which means that this donkey had never been ridden before. This donkey was one that was supposed to be for the coming Messiah. When Christ did this, He was fulfilling prophecy found in Zechariah 9:9, where it says, *"Rejoice greatly, daughter Zion! Shout, Daughter Jerusalem! See, you King comes to you, righteous and victorious, lowly and riding on a donkey, on a colt, the foal of a donkey."* **4**

Going Deeper Response

USE A BIBLE CONCORDANCE OR BIBLE DICTIONARY AND LOOK UP THE WORDS WORSHIP & REVERENCE FOR STUDY

Pray: Asking God to help us have the same mindset...

_____

Lesson written by Pastor Frank & Samuel Gervasi

1. Wikipedia, https://en.wikipedia.org/wiki/Washington_Monument, as accessed on 11/03/2024.
2. Grace to You, https://www.gty.org/library/sermons-library/81-42/the-humble-coronation-of-king-jesus, as accessed on 11/03/2024.
3. *Inspiring Worship Quotes,* https://mediashout.com/19-inspiring-worship-quotes-2025/, as accessed on 04/08/2025.
4. New International Bible, Holy Bible, New International Version®, NIV® Copyright ©1973, 1978, 1984, 2011 by Biblica, Inc.® Used by permission. All rights reserved worldwide.

Lesson 2 – Membership is Not a Country Club

Memory Verse: *"Consequently, you are no longer foreigners and strangers, but fellow citizens with God's people and also members of his household.'"* **Ephesians 2:19, NIV**

Open in Prayer:

Introduction:

Church membership has been said by some to be a very valuable tool for growing in faith. However, it really has been a misunderstood topic in many churches and believers across the country. In fact, it was recently reported that church membership has gone down 19% in the last sixteen years. Which is really a big number that has ramifications for the Spiritual maturity of many people, including the ones that were not part of this research.

Read: *Ephesians 2:19-22*

"Consequently, you are no longer foreigners and strangers, but fellow citizens with God's people and also members of his household, 20 built on the foundation of the apostles and prophets, with Christ Jesus himself as the chief cornerstone. 21 In him the whole building is joined together and rises to become a holy temple in the Lord. 22 And in him you too are being built together to become a dwelling in which God lives by his Spirit." (NIV)

<u>Big Idea:</u> *Christians become a part of a bigger family, and believers are growing and becoming a Holy Temple where God's Spirit Dwells.*

The apostle Paul when addressing the church at Ephesus wasn't necessarily correcting any bad or erroneous behaviors, or interpersonal issues with anyone. Rather he was giving, in part, a sound model for the type of relationships that should exist after a person becomes a Christ follower.

1. *What Could Be Some Benefits to Being a Member of a Local Church?*
   a. _____
   b. _____
   c. _____

In verse 19 he describes being, "members of Christ's household." Even though he may have been referring to Gentiles being included into God's family, he is also saying that we are *part "of a family with Christ as the head." 2* (verse 20.)

2. Do I View Other Christians as My Family? *(Explain Your Answer)*

_____
_____
_____
_____

Many times, people think that Church membership is not in the Bible. However, the concept is woven through the New Testament and one of the most important tools that God uses to grow us and His church.

Now, the word itself (membership) is not found many times in that form. Nevertheless, in the book of Acts alone, approximately 82% of the passages regarding becoming a Christian are referring to the local body of believers and NOT the Universal Christian Church. There are approximately 17 references to where a person was added to the church. About 14 out of the 17 are giving an image of believers becoming part of a local congregation. That's not counting the epistles where the concept is also being modelled in the context of the local church.

3. *What Are Some Benefits to Having People Close to me From Church?*

a. _____

b. _____

c. _____

d. _____

4. *What Are Some Downfalls to Allowing People Close to Me?*

_____

_____

_____

<u>**Insight:**</u> *Membership is a tool that God uses to grow each member into a family. Built on the principles of the Apostles with Christ as the Chief Cornerstone. Membership is a covenant between individual believers and a local church of commitment, where individuals and churches grow into a place where Christ's Spirit dwells.*

Family relationships are always growing and changing over time. However, ultimately, we become a place where Christ's Spirit can dwell. Verse 29 says that *"we are becoming a holy temple for the Lord."* **1**

Obviously, the Scriptures show the importance of being connected to each other through a local body of believers, even though the actual term might not be there.

5. *What Do the Following Verses Show About Families?*

John 8:35	
Acts 7:20	
Acts 10:2	
Galatians 6:10	

What mindsets get in the way of being a good member of my local church?

a. _____

b. _____

c. _____

What ways can I grow in the areas I serve? _____

_____

_____

_____

What ways could hinder God's Spirit dwelling in me? _____

_____

_____

_____

Going Deeper:

Member, even though the Greek word is not found in the New Testament. The concept of it is an important one and word. In the Old Testament it may not have been as imperative because Jewish life was centered around the Synagogue. They studied, went to school, served, and were instructed in the Torah. So, the idea of community was almost expected and just assumed. However, in the New Testament the concept of Membership became very important because the church was a new concept. As well as conflict that arose between orthodox Jews and the Christian Church. In fact, some of *"the times that the word is used in the New Testament refers to the organs of a body, as well as a part of the whole."* Especially in places like Matthew *5:29, Romans 6:13, Romans 7:23, Romans 12:4, and 1 Corinthians 12:12-27.* Which is important because Christ viewed the church as members of a body intricately connected to Himself. *Membership is a covenant between individual believers and a local church of commitment, where individuals and churches grow into a place where Christ's Spirit dwells.* **2**

Going Deeper Response

LOCATE EVERY TIME IN THE BOOK OF ACTS THAT REFERERS TO THE CHURCH & COUNT HOW MANY ARE SPEAKING OF THE LOCAL OR UNIVERSAL CHURCH

**Pray:** *Asking God to make my life a place where His Spirit would want to dwell....*

Lesson written by Pastor Frank & Samuel Gervasi

Works Cited:

1. New International Version (NIV), Holy Bible, New International Version®, NIV® Copyright ©1973, 1978, 1984, 2011 by Biblica, Inc.® Used by permission. All rights reserved worldwide.
2. J. Knox, An Interpreter's Dictionary of the Bible, Abington Press, Copyright 1962.

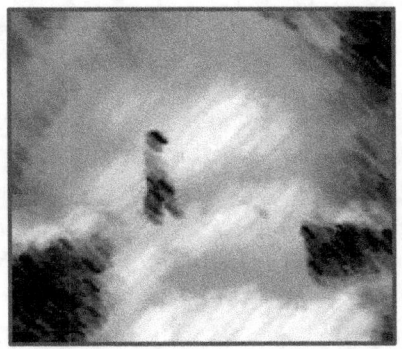

Lesson 3 - Benefits of Strong Faith

Memory Verse: *"The Royal Official said, 'Sir, come down before my child dies.' 'Go,' Jesus replied, 'your son will live.'"* **John 4:49-50, NIV**

Open in Prayer:

Introduction:

The dictionary defines faith as: "the ability to trust in the worth or ability of someone or something." 1 However, it really is a great definition even though it's a secular one. Because it relates to matters of faith as well. Both in the concepts of belief in God ---- Himself, and belief in what the Scriptures tell us as well. Now, in the case of having trust in God, a person needs to accept who He says He is, fully and completely. Additionally, though it's also true because a person must believe completely how the Bible commands, encourages, and exhorts us to live. Nevertheless, that's not such an easy thing to do sometimes, is it? Especially when you think about all the variables that come into play with life at times. Nevertheless, faith is a key ingredient needed for maximum growth regardless of how long a person has been walking with Christ.

Read: *John 4:46-54*

"Once more he visited Cana in Galilee, where he had turned the water into wine. And there was a certain royal official whose son lay sick at Capernaum. 47 When this man heard that Jesus had arrived in Galilee from Judea, he went to him and begged him to come and heal his son, who was close to death. 48 'Unless you people see signs and wonders,' Jesus told him, 'you will never believe.' 49 The

royal official said, 'Sir, come down before my child dies.' 50 'Go,' Jesus replied, 'your son will live.' The man took Jesus at his word and departed.'"

"'51 While he was still on the way, his servants met him with the news that his boy was living. 52 When he inquired as to the time when his son got better, they said to him, 'Yesterday, at one in the afternoon, the fever left him.' 53 Then the father realized that this was the exact time at which Jesus had said to him, 'Your son will live.' So, he and his whole household believed. 54 This was the second sign Jesus performed after coming from Judea to Galilee." (NIV).

Big Idea: *Faith is required for all the seasons of a Christ-follower's life if they want to experience God's best in life.*

Faith in *God* **and** His *abilities* is required for **all** the Christian life, from beginning to end. For both *young* and *old*, both *small* and *big*, -for the newly saved to those who've been following Christ for several years. As well as, from the *smallest* thing, ---to the *biggest* thing we really need God for everything.

If you look at the context of the passage it was very simple for the healing of the Royal Official's son. Even though it doesn't tell us *what* the sickness was, it was definitely a *serious issue* because it says he was *"close to death." (v.47.)*

1. ***Do I believe God Heals in Dramatic Ways like in the passage?*** *(Explain your answers)* _____
   _____
   _____
   _____

2. ***What Mindsets/Thoughts Get in the Way of Having Faith That God Can Do the Miraculous in My Life?*** *(Be Thorough)*
   a. _____
   b. _____
   c. _____
   d. _____

What's clear is that the official believed **fully** that Jesus could do the miraculous in his son's life. Because v. 47 says *"He went and begged"* **2** Christ for healing. Now, it could have been out of *desperation*, but most likely, it was because he had heard and maybe even seen second hand about all Christ had been doing. The miracles performed, the teaching with authority, and even challenging long held beliefs of the leaders of that day and culture.

Even Though God *Cares* About *Everything*—Christ's *First* Concern is a Person's *Soul*. Consider that, because He doesn't care more about your *health* than your final destination. He doesn't care about your *wealth* more than your soul. And He doesn't care about your *relationships* more than the place in eternity either! What Jesus **does** care about *most* is whether you've come to a place of repentance, and whether you've received the forgiveness that comes from embracing the Cross. (John 3:16.)

3. **Why Would God Care So Much About a Person's Soul?** *(Be Specific)* _____

_____
_____
_____

_____

Insight: *Belief is really required for all needs in the Christian life. If you have a need, trust fully that God can do whatever is needed for you. Whether it's a minor relationship issue, are facing a major decision, or are at the receiving end of a major health scare.*

_____

4. **In What Ways Do I Limit God in My Life?** *(Explain Your Answers.)*

a. _____ b. _____
b. _____ d. _____

In verse 48 it *says "'Unless you people see signs and wonders,' Jesus told him, 'You will never believe.'"* **2** Even though Christ doesn't say that specifically, that is what was being referred to. Because the *signs and wonders* that people would see, were just the signs that He was the Son of God, that was to come into the World. The Kingdom of God had finally arrived.

5. What Do the Following Verses Say About Faith?

Genesis 5:24	
Genesis 17:1-4	
2 Chronicles 20:20	
Mathew 6:30	
Luke 5:20	

"If you believe in a God who controls the big things, you must believe in God who controls the little things. It is we of course to whom things look little or big." 3 Elliott

---

Challenge Section:

What is My Level of Faith Currently? (Rate Yourself 1-10-Explain Your Reasoning)

_____

_____

_____

What Areas Have I Allowed My Faith to Weaken?

_____

_____

_____

What Practical Things Can I Do to Grow in Faith?

a. _____

b. _____

c. _____

Going Deeper:

There's also another reason that shows the Royal Official had great faith. And that is, *because* he was said to have worked for Herod Antipas, the son of Herod the Great. Even though that doesn't sound like it's significant.it really is! Because he was *most likely* **not** very fond of Christ ---being raised around all that *jealously and animosity* towards Christ. In fact, Pilate sent Christ back to Antipas, and he was mocked and sent back and forth. So, the Royal Official that was asking for a miracle was used to hearing nothing but negative talk about Jesus. All that to say, that he was showing great belief in who Christ was saying that He was! The ***NIV Study Bible*** adds *"unless you see signs and wonders you will never believe." Was the general attitude of Galileans, not that of the official."* **4**

Going Deeper Response
READ HEBREWS 11 - HALL OF FAITH CHAPTER, AND LIST EVERY PERSON THE WRITER BRINGS UP FOR HAVING FAITH.

<u>*Pray:*</u> *Asking God to stretch my faith in Him, so that I can experience Him in a greater way....*

———————

Lesson written by Pastor Frank & Samuel Gervasi

———————

<u>Works Cited:</u>

1. Webster's Dictionary, Merriam-Webster, Inc, 2016
2. New International Version (NIV), Holy Bible, New International Version®, NIV® Copyright ©1973, 1978, 1984, 2011 by Biblica, Inc.® Used by permission. All rights reserved worldwide.
3. Jungle Pilot, Russel Hilt, Discovery House Publishers, 1997
4. NIV Study Bible, BibleGatewayPlus, Biblegateway.com, as accessed on 03/20/2025

Lesson 4 – Praying Like a Disciple

Memory Verse: *"One day Jesus was praying in a certain place. When he finished, one of his disciples said to him, 'Lord, teach us to pray, just as John taught his disciples.'"* **Luke 11:1, NIV**

Open In Prayer

Introduction:

Our prayer life is probably one of the most important things that we can do! That true because it's one of the most basic disciplines for the Christian, and every follower needs to do it. But prayer can be one that is also a misunderstood and under-taught topics in some churches. Additionally, it doesn't matter how long you've been a Christian because no one seems to graduate from the necessity of prayer. Christ himself, realized the importance of it and prayed often. You see prayer is the thing that makes our faith real. It takes us from just mere head knowledge to actually living out the Christian faith. Some people pray often - and for long periods of time, but for others, it's small, short, one-line prayers - as they're going about their day. However, both types of people understand the importance of praying on a regular basis.

Read: *Luke 11:1-4*

"'One day Jesus was praying in a certain place. When he finished, one of his disciples said to him, 'Lord, teach us to pray, just as John taught his disciples.' 2 He said to them, 'When you pray, say: Father, hallowed be your name, your kingdom come. 3 Give us each day our daily bread. 4 Forgive us our sins, for we

also forgive everyone who sins against us. And lead us not into temptation.'"
(NIV)

Big Idea: *Prayer is Critical and Should Be Inspiring When Pray Like a True Disciple*

The passage we are studying today is between an encounter between Jesus and His disciples regarding prayer. They had all been influenced and experienced Jesus praying daily and in various ways and with various requests. (v. 1.) So, after finishing one day his disciples ask to be taught about prayer. (v.1.) They had also experienced John the Baptist pray, as well as teach his own followers. There must have been something compelling about seeing Jesus pray or they probably wouldn't have asked. If you think about it: They grew up going to the synagogue, so they had seen people pray often. Meaning, it wasn't foreign to them. In fact, they had probably grown up and were accustomed to praying.

1. **What Are Some Possible Reasons People Can Sometimes Avoid Prayer?** *(Explain)* _____
    _____
    _____

2. **What Do the Following Verses Say About Prayer?**

Exodus 9:29	
1 Samuel 2:1	
2 Samuel 7:27	
Romans 1:9-10	
Romans 12:12	

3. **What Specific Areas Can We Pray For?** *(Explain Your Answers)*
    a. _____ *b.* _____
    c. _____ *d.* _____
    e. _____ *f.* _____

One of the most popular prayers in scripture is what's known as the Lord's Prayer. Which is exactly what Christ chose to teach His disciples when asked to be taught as John the Baptist's disciples were taught. (v. 2.) *However,* giving a model or standard for prayer as opposed to actual prayer to be verbatim. In verse 2 he says: *"Father, hallowed be your name,"* **1** showing that we should remember who we are coming before when we pray. *"Thy kingdom come,"* implying that we should be longing for God's kingdom to be realized here on Earth during our lifetime. And prayer should also be for daily provision in life, (v.3,) when he says, *"Give us this day our daily bread."* As well as forgiveness when we fail, or others fail us. In v. 4 it says: *"Forgive us our sins, for we also forgive everyone who sins against us."* **1** As well as praying for strength against life's temptation (v. 4.)

I was taught the same prayer at a young age. I always knew the words, but something seemed to be missing in the reciting of the Lord's Prayer. The actual pattern that was behind it seemed to be replaced with repetition of the words only.

Insight: *Consider having a prayer life that others want to emulate. It is probably one of the most encouraging things that shows our prayer life, when done correctly, can inspire others and be contagious.*

---

4. ***When is Your Ideal Time and Format to Pray?*** *(Explain Why and Give an Example)*

_____

_____

_____

"Get up to your chamber, then, if you would have a broken and contrite spirit and come not out until you have it." John Bradford 2

John Bradford the English Reformer, prebendary of St. Paul's, and martyr said that, when he was in prayer, he never liked to rise from his knees till he began to feel something of brokenness of heart.

Going Deeper:

The Greek term father as used in the New Testament is an understood one to the audience that Luke was reaching initially. However, the term Abba was probably more well known.

Abba was Aramaic in origin and said to be a term of endearment and closeness.
So, for Jesus to use it, may have been saying that we can come freely and abandon ourselves before God the Father when we bring our requests. Even the *Zondervan Illustrated Bible Backgrounds Commentary of the New Testament* addresses that: *"While it has been commonly said that Abba is a children's term meaning "daddy," this is not quite right, since Jewish adults also addressed their parents in this way. Abba was, however, a term of considerable intimacy. While Jews would sometimes refer to God as "our heavenly Father," they rarely if ever addressed him as "my father" or*

"father" (Abba). Jesus calls his followers to a new intimacy with God through his unique relationship with the Father." 3

Pray: Asking God to stretch my prayer life, so that I can experience Him in a fresh way....

———————————

Lesson written by Pastor Frank & Samuel Gervasi

———————————

Works Cited:

1. New International Version (NIV), Holy Bible, ® Copyright ©1973, 1978, 1984, 2011 by Biblica, Inc.® Used by permission. All rights reserved worldwide.
2. Sermon Central Contributor, www.sermoncentral.com, as accessed on 03/20/2025
3. Zondervan Illustrated Bible Backgrounds Commentary of the New Testament, Copyright © 2002

Lesson 5 - Trust and Obey

Memory Verse: *"So. Abraham called that place The Lord Will Provide. And to this day it is said, 'On the mountain of the Lord it will be provided.'"* **Genesis 22:14, NIV**

Open in Prayer:

Introduction:

Sometimes, obedience is costly and defies logic. During the Prussian siege of Paris in the late 1800s, there was a gunner in one of the French forts named Pierre Barlot. One day, Pierre was standing by his gun when General Noel, his commander, said to him, "Gunner, do you see the Sevres bridge over there?" "Yes, sir." "And that little shanty in a thicket of shrubs to the left of the bridge?" "I see it, sir," said Pierre. "It's full of Prussians, I believe; try it with a shell." Pierre turned ghostly pale. He sighted his cannon carefully, then fired it, and blew the hut to shreds. The commander Noel praised Pierre for his marksmanship but was surprised to see a single tear running down the gunner's cheek. "What's the matter, man?" "Pardon me, General," said Pierre, "it was my house—everything I had in the world." 1

Read: *Genesis 22:1-18*

*"Some time later God tested Abraham. He said to him, "Abraham!" "Here I am,"
he replied. 2 Then God said, "Take your son, your only son, whom you love—
Isaac—and go to the region of Moriah. Sacrifice him there as a burnt offering on
a mountain I will show you." 3 Early the next morning Abraham got up and
loaded his donkey. He took with him two of his servants and his son Isaac. When
he had cut enough wood for the burnt offering, he set out for the place God had*

told him about. 4 On the third day Abraham looked up and saw the place in the distance.

5 He said to his servants, "Stay here with the donkey while I and the boy go over there. We will worship and then we will come back to you." 6 Abraham took the wood for the burnt offering and placed it on his son Isaac, and he himself carried the fire and the knife. As the two of them went on together, 7 Isaac spoke up and said to his father Abraham, "Father?" "Yes, my son?" Abraham replied. "The fire and wood are here," Isaac said, "but where is the lamb for the burnt offering?" 8 Abraham answered, "God himself will provide the lamb for the burnt offering, my son." And the two of them went on together. 9 When they reached the place God had told him about, Abraham built an altar there and arranged the wood on it. He bound his son Isaac and laid him on the altar, on top of the wood. 10 Then he reached out his hand and took the knife to slay his son. 11 But the angel of the Lord called out to him from heaven, "Abraham! Abraham!" "Here I am," he replied. 12 "Do not lay a hand on the boy," he said. "Do not do anything to him. Now I know that you fear God, because you have not withheld from me your son, your only son." 13 Abraham looked up and there in a thicket he saw a ram[a] caught by its horns. He went over and took the ram and sacrificed it as a burnt offering instead of his son. 14 So Abraham called that place The Lord Will Provide. And to this day it is said, "On the mountain of the Lord it will be provided." 15 The angel of the Lord called to Abraham from heaven a second time 16 and said, "I swear by myself, declares the Lord, that because you have done this and have not withheld your son, your only son, 17 I will surely bless you and make your descendants as numerous as the stars in the sky and as the sand on the seashore. Your descendants will take possession of the cities of their enemies, 18 and through your offspring[b] all nations on earth will be blessed, because you have obeyed me." (NIV)

Big Idea: *Faith in God, proven by deliberate and complete obedience, will always be compensated in due time.*

God commanded Abraham to show a similarly great depth of faith in what some have called Abraham's "final exam". There was no softening of the blow when God spoke to Abraham clearly in verses 2-3: "'*Take your son, your only son, whom you love – Isaac – and...sacrifice him there as a burnt offering.'*"

Don't forget how everything that God had promised Abraham about his descendants was going to be fulfilled through Isaac. Isaac was himself a miracle, considering the age at which Abraham and his wife Sarah gave birth to him. Then God is asking Abraham to sacrifice the child who was the very fulfillment of His promise years earlier.

1. **What Does it Mean to Sacrifice Something?** *(Explain Your Answer)* ____
_____
_____
_____
_____

2. **What Do You Think God Wants you to Sacrifice to Grow in Faith?** (Be Specific)
a. _____ b. _____
c. _____ d. _____

What God asked Abraham to do does not sound, in our day and age, like good fatherly advice. In fact, you might receive a visit from Family Services for child-rearing like this! And yet, Abraham responds with deliberate, decisive, and complete obedience. Notice that Abraham rose "early the next morning" (v. 3). Abraham did not hesitantly delay doing what God said, he was quick and decisive to trust and obey from the moment God told him to sacrifice Isaac, his own son!

3. **Look Up the Following Verses and Write Down What Character Trait Stands Out?**

Genesis 3:13	
Psalm 109:16	
Proverbs 23:24	
Luke 11:11-13	

Additionally, Abraham is tested for his faith in this passage. He believes God at His Word and trusts Him fully, and, in response, God rewards Abraham for his faith. First, God provides a way out of the demanding situation by providing a ram in a thicket *"caught by its horns"* (v. 13) to be sacrificed in Isaac's place. At the very last moment, when Abraham is about to go through with the unimaginable, God provides a way out.

4. What Are Reasons Obedience Can Be Hard at Times?

a. _____   b. _____

c. _____   d. _____

e. _____   f. _____

Then finally, God Himself rewards Abraham's faithfulness by renewing the covenant in verses16-18: *"'I swear by myself, declares the LORD, that because you have done this and not withheld your son, your only son, I will surely bless you and make your descendants as numerous as the stars in the sky…and through your offspring all nations on earth will be blessed, because you have obeyed me.'"*

Insight: *Faith and obedience are inseparable: one cannot claim to take God at His word if he or she is not willing to do what God has said. When we say that we have faith in God, we must obey His commands.*

---

5. Look Up the Following Verses and Describe How God Responded to Their Faithfulness?

Genesis 15:1-6	
Numbers 22:17	
Ruth 2:12	
1 Samuel 26:23	
Psalm 19:11	
Colossians 3:24	

God may never ask us to trust Him for something so great. But He does ask all of us, at various times, to trust Him for something. And complete faith, proven by obedience, will always be compensated in due time.

*What Areas of My Life is God Asking Me to Have Faith With?*_____

_____

_____

*What can I Do to Grow in Trusting and Obeying God?*_____

_____

_____

*What Have I Been Withholding from God?*_____

_____

_____

Going Deeper:

In Hebrews 11, the Hall of Faith, Abraham is one of those commended for his faith in verses 17-19: *"By faith Abraham, when he was tested, offered up Isaac; and he who received the promises was offering up his only begotten son; it was he to whom it was said, 'In Isaac your seed shall be called.' He that considered that God is able to raise men even from the dead."*

The **NIV Study Bible** says regarding these verses:
"If you are afraid to trust God with your most prized possession, dream, or person, pay attention to Abraham's example. Because Abraham was willing to give up everything for God, he received back more than he could have imagined." **2**

Going Deeper Response

FIND A BIBLE COMMENTARY AND LOOK UP GENESIS 22:1-18

Pray: Asking God to help me trust Him no matter the circumstances and obey fully no matter how difficult.

Lesson written by Pastor Frank & Samuel Gervasi

———————

1. Ministry127, https://ministry127.com/resources/illustration/the-cost-of-obedience, as accessed on 08/25/2024.
2. Zondervan NIV Life Application Study Bible. Ronald A Beers, gen. ed. Zondervan. Copyright 2011

Lesson 6 – Forgiveness is Not Optional

Memory Verse: *"Then Peter came to Jesus and asked, 'Lord, how many times shall I forgive my brother or sister who sins against me? Up to seven times?'"* **Matthew 18:21, NIV**

Open in Prayer:

Introduction

Just before Easter in 2009, Fred Winters, pastor of the First Baptist Church in Maryville, Illinois, was shot and killed during a Sunday morning service by a disturbed young man. The tragedy shocked the church and the pastor's family, but it did not destroy their faith. The next week the newly widowed Cindy Winters was interviewed on a national news broadcast. When asked about her husband's killer she said, *"I do not have any hatred or even hard feelings toward him. We have been praying for him."* [1] We may never have to forgive someone for something so tragic, but we are *ALL* called to forgive at one time or another.

Read: *Matthew 18:21-35*

"Then Peter came to Jesus and asked, 'Lord, how many times shall I forgive my brother or sister who sins against me? Up to seven times?' 22 Jesus answered, 'I tell you, not seven times, but seventy-seven times.' 23 'Therefore, the kingdom of heaven is like a king who wanted to settle accounts with his servants. 24 As he began the settlement, a man who owed him ten thousand bags of gold was brought to him. 25 Since he was not able to pay, the master ordered that he and his wife and his children and all that he had be sold to repay the debt. 26 'At this the servant fell on his knees before him. "Be patient with me," he begged, "and I will pay back everything."

27 The servant's master took pity on him, canceled the debt and let him go. 28 'But when that servant went out, he found one of his fellow servants who owed him a hundred silver coins. He grabbed him and began to choke him. "Pay back what you owe me!" he demanded. 29 'His fellow servant fell to his knees and begged him, "Be patient with me, and I will pay it back." 30 'But he refused. Instead, he went off and had the man thrown into prison until he could pay the debt. 31 When the other servants saw what had happened, they were outraged and went and told their master everything that had happened. 32 'Then the master called the servant in. "You wicked servant," he said, "I canceled all that debt of yours because you begged me to. 33 Shouldn't you have had mercy on your fellow servant just as I had on you?" 34 In anger his master handed him over to the jailers to be tortured, until he should pay back all he owed. 35 'This is how my heavenly Father will treat each of you unless you forgive your brother or sister from your heart.'" **NIV**

Big Idea: Forgiveness is not optional and costly and will require something of us to pardon others when they have hurt us.

In today's Bible passage, we see a parable where Peter asks Jesus an important question regarding forgiveness. *"Then Peter came to Jesus and asked, 'Lord, how many times shall I forgive my brother or sister who sins against me? Up to seven times?'"* (v. 21, NIV)

Even though it sounds like a straightforward question, it may have been rooted in what was taught during those times. The main teaching by Jewish leaders regarding forgiveness, was that a person could be forgiven up to three times to fulfill Mosaic Law. So, for Peter to ask up to seven times may have been a way to seem *ultra-spiritual* before his mentor.

1. How Easy, or Difficult, Is It for You to Forgive Someone When They Have Wronged You? *(Explain)*

_____

_____

_____

_____

However, Jesus raises the bar for His followers by giving such a large number. In verse 22 it says that, *"Jesus answered,*

'I tell you, not seven times, but seventy-seven times.'"
Which was an even bigger number than what many were used to hearing. Implying that God doesn't want us to keep track of how many times we forgive others.

2. What Might Be Some Reasons It's Difficult to Forgive Someone Multiple Times for the Same Offense? *(Be Specific)*

a. _____

b. _____

c. _____

d. _____

Additionally, another aspect regarding forgiveness is that it usually will cost us something when a person makes the choice to forgive an offense. Whether that hurt is just the financial cost of a real debt, or an emotional debt from being hurt.

In the parable, Jesus tells of a king that wanted to settle an account of a servant that owed him about twenty years of a day-laborer's wages and could not pay (vv. 23-24). Nevertheless, when the servant could not pay the debt and he begged the king to forgive the debt, he was released (v. 25).

3. What Do the Following Verses Say/Show About Forgiveness:

Genesis 45:4-8	
2 Samuel 19:18-23	
1 Kings 21:27-29	
Micah 7:18	
Ephesians 4:32	

4. What Might It Cost Us to Forgive Others? *(Explain your Answer)*

_____
_____
_____
_____

When the servant was put in a similar situation, for an even smaller amount, he did not forgive the person who was indebted to him. Instead, he went and had him thrown into prison until the debt could be paid, as we see in verses 28-30, *"But when that servant went out, he found one of his fellow servants who owed him a hundred silver coins...'Pay back what you owe me!' he demanded...But he refused. Instead, he went off and had the man thrown in prison until he could pay the debt."*

5. Why Might We Fail to Show Forgiveness to Others? *(Explain Your Answers)* _____
_____
_____

Jesus paid the price for our forgiveness with the high price of death on a Cross. We should also reciprocate and forgive others!

6. What Do the Following Verses Show About God's Forgiveness Toward Us?

Psalm 103:12	
Nehemiah 9:17	
John 3:17	
Romans 5:8	

"What sets Christians apart from the world is the obligation and compulsion to forgive."
Author Unknown

Challenge Section

Who do I need to forgive for an offense? _____
_____

Do I give out forgiveness freely, or tend to withhold it? Yes or No (Circle One) (Explain Your Answer)
_____
_____
_____

Am I keeping count of when someone wrongs me? _____
_____
_____

Going Deeper:

The Talmud, which was the central rabbinic teaching for Judaism, instructed that people were to forgive up to three times. However, after that there was no longer an obligation to forgive another individual. At least in what was required when obeying Mosaic Law. The **NIV Grace and Truth Study Bible** says, *"Within Judaism, forgiving someone three times was enough to show a forgiving spirit (Job 33:29–30; Am 1:3; 2:6). Peter's suggestion seven times shows generosity. Jesus' response is not about a specific number but is an instruction to forgive without keeping count.*

He illustrates this with a parable in which a servant owes his king an incalculable debt, at least 2.5 billion dollars in today's terms. The point is the immensity of the debt and the impossibility of paying it back. The king orders that the servant and all he has be sold into debtor's slavery, a common practice in the ancient world that was designed both as a punishment and as a means to repayment (cf. 2Ki 4:1; Ne 5:4–8)." [2] Additionally, some versions of the Bible say seventy-times-seven which is a large number, even much more generous than the seven times Peter suggested. However, some manuscripts suggest that it was seventy times seven which is four hundred and ninety times.

Going Deeper Response

USE A BIBLE CONCORDANCE OR BIBLE DICTIONARY AND LOOK UP THE WORD FORGIVENESS FOR STUDY

Pray: Asking God to help us forgive no matter the circumstances and not matter how many times we have been hurt...

_____

Lesson written by Pastor Frank & Samuel Gervasi

_____

Works Cited:

1. Ministry127, *https://ministry127.com/resources/illustrations/forgiveness,* as accessed on 3/20/2025.
2. *NIV Grace and Truth Study Bible*, Copyright © 2021 by Zondervan, 2011. *BibleGateway Plus*, www.biblegateway.com, as accessed on 3/20/2025.
3. New International Bible, Holy Bible, New International Version®, NIV® Copyright ©1973, 1978, 1984, 2011 by Biblica, Inc.® Used by permission. All rights reserved worldwide.

Lesson 7 – Enduring Prayer

Memory Verse: *"Ask, and it will be given to you; seek and you will find; knock and the door will be opened to you."* **Matthew 7:7, NIV**

Open in Prayer:

Introduction

A fisherman was at sea with his godless companions when a storm came up and threatened to sink their ship. His friends begged him to pray; but he said, *"It's been a long time since I've done that or even entered a church."* At their insistence, however, he finally cried out, *"O Lord, I haven't asked anything of You in 15 years, and if You help us now and bring us safely to land, I promise I won't bother you again for another 15!"*

Unfortunately, many people view prayer as an escape mechanism rather than a constant line of communication with God. **1** Prayer is necessary for our relationship with God. However, when the answer is long in coming, we should still continue to pray.

Read: *Luke 18:1-8*

"Then Jesus told his disciples a parable to show them that they should always pray and not give up. 2 He said: 'In a certain town there was a judge who neither feared God nor cared what people thought. 3 And there was a widow in that town who kept coming to him with the plea, "Grant me justice against my adversary." 4 'For some time he refused. But finally he said to himself, "Even though I don't fear God or care what people think, 5 yet because this widow keeps bothering me, I will see that she gets justice, so that she won't eventually come and attack me!"' 6 And the Lord said, 'Listen to what the unjust judge says. 7 And will not God bring about justice for his chosen ones, who cry out to him day and night? Will he keep putting them off? 8 I tell you, he will see that they get justice, and quickly. However, when the Son of Man comes, will he find faith on the earth?'" **(NIV)**

Big Idea: We should be persistent in prayer and never give up even when the request is a long time in being answered.

---

1. Who is Someone You Know Who Never Gives Up? (Give an Example) __

_____
_____
_____

The passage we're looking at is from the Gospel of Luke. And in it, Jesus was teaching about never giving up in prayer, and how to persevere over time when we need to. So, he does this by telling a parable to make His point, involving an unjust judge and a widow. So, there are many variables that come into play as well.

First, Jesus was teaching a parable to His disciples. However, He was obviously speaking to all people who call themselves Christ followers and would later read this. Additionally, we also know that parables are stories used to teach spiritual truth. So maybe they happened, maybe not, but it doesn't really matter anyway when it comes to applying them to our lives.

2. What Might Be Some Reasons God Takes So Long to Answer Our Prayers?

a. _____
b. _____
c. _____
d. _____

We saw that the story contained some main characters, like a judge, a widow, and an unnamed adversary. (vv. 1-3.) We read in v. 2 *"That there was a certain judge who neither feared God nor cared about men."* Which I think says a lot about this judge's mindset because he really didn't seem to care about what this widow even needed. That mindset is much different than our God because He is One who cares intimately about all that concerns us always.

However, something that I think stands out is the widow's request. Because Luke records the term *"adversary"*.

Verse 3 says: *"And there was a widow in that town who kept coming to him with the plea, 'Grant me justice against my adversary.'"*

One version uses the word *opponent* – which is an interesting word because it carries this idea of an opponent much like in a lawsuit. Which explains why she was going to a judge in the first place: to seek justice from the unjust judge. (v. 2.)

3. *What Do the Following Verses Show Us About Prayer:*

1 Kings 18:39-46	
Ezra 8:23	
Jeremiah 33:3	
John 15:5-8	
Colossians 4:2-4	

Nevertheless, the Judge was not fair or even concerned about the people in general. So why would this judge help the widow?
Regardless of the details, he did grant her request because of her tenacity and

Insight: *We should pray with determination and perseverance because it keeps us focused on the need, especially when the answer is long.*

---

persistence. (vv. 4-5.) *""Even though I do not fear God nor respect man, yet because this widow bothers me, I will give her legal protection, otherwise by continually coming she will wear me out.""* (NASB 1995)

4. Why Might We <u>Not</u> Pray with Persistence When the Answer Is a Long Time in Coming? *(Explain your Answer)* _____

_____

_____

_____

"We should pray, then pray more, and after that pray even more." Author Unknown

---

So, if the unjust judge will grant justice, how much more will God hear the prayers of His children? God longs to give His best to us, so we should come freely and with abandon before His throne.

5. **How Might It Look for Us to Pray with Abandon?** *(Explain Your Answers)*

_____
_____
_____

We may not need a judge to decide a case for us, but we all have needs of one variety or another. Regardless of what those are, endurance is usually needed, and we would be wise in being persistent in prayer.

6. **What Do the Following Verses Show About God Answering Our Prayers?**

Psalm 18:6	
Proverbs 15:8	
2 Chronicles 7:14	
Mark 11:23-25	

Challenge

On a scale of 1 to 10, how persistent am I in prayer? (1 being the lowest, 10 the highest)

1 – ---------------2.5------------------ 5 -------------------7.5------------------10

Do I easily give up when the wait is long? Yes or No (Circle One) (Explain Your Answer)

_____
_____
_____

What are some ways I can train myself to be persistent in prayer? _____

_____
_____

Going Deeper:

Consider the widow in the parable because they were said to be very needy in that time and culture. Much different than today because widows are very independent and do many things for themselves. In fact, we have widows today, and they take care of themselves perfectly fine. However, in that day, widows were very dependent on others just like in this parable. One source says: *"The widow was a helpless person with nothing but right on her side. She wanted justice, not revenge."* (ESV Reformation Study Bible, Ligonier, 2015) **2**

Additionally, the **Expositor's Bible Commentary** says, *"The theme is that of the vindication of God's misunderstood and suffering people. God's people in the OT days needed to "wait" on God as he worked out justice with apparent slowness (see Ps. 25:2-3). In the final days the martyrs wait for vindication (Rev 6:9-11). Meanwhile we wrestle with the problem of evil and with issues of theodicy. Under these circumstances we should 'always pray and not give up.'"* **3**

Going Deeper Response
USE A BIBLE TO LOOK UP THREE CHARACTERS IN THE SCRIPTURES WHO PRAYED PERSISTENTLY. READ THEIR STORIES AND WRITE DOWN THE LESSONS YOU CAN LEARN ABOUT PRAYER FROM THEIR LIVES.

Pray: Asking God to give us the endurance we need to pray over the long haul when needed...

_____

Lesson written by Pastor Frank & Samuel Gervasi

_____

Works Cited:

1. Ministry127, *https://ministry127.com/resources/illustrations/prayer,* as accessed on 3/20/2025.
2. *ESV Reformation Study Bible,* Copyright © 2015 by Ligonier. *BibleGateway Plus, www.biblegateway.com,* as accessed on 3/20/2025.

3. *Expositor's Bible Commentary* (Abridged Edition): New Testament, Copyright © 2004. BibleGateway Plus, *www.biblegateway.com*, as accessed on 3/20/2025.
4. New International Bible, Holy Bible, New International Version®, NIV® Copyright ©1973, 1978, 1984, 2011 by Biblica, Inc.® Used by permission. All rights reserved worldwide.

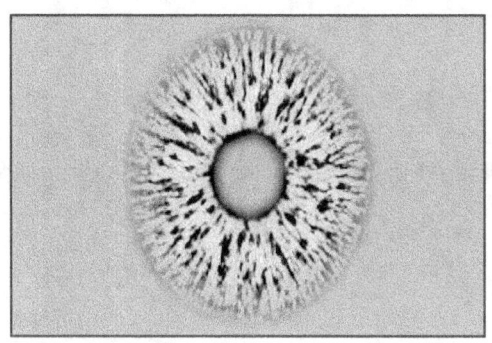

Lesson 8 – Eye in the Sky

Memory Verse: *"The LORD will watch over your coming and going both now and forevermore."* **Psalm 121:8, NIV**

Open in Prayer:

Introduction

King salmon, also known as Chinook salmon, lead an incredible life. After spending most of their lives in the ocean, Chinook salmon embark on a migration back to the same freshwater streams where they were born to lay their own eggs. This journey often covers several thousand miles and requires the salmon to swim against the strong force of the current. Yet every year, thousands can be seen swimming in a caravan to go back to the place they were born.

The Israelites often made a similarly difficult journey, albeit of a shorter distance. Every year, the Israelites would come up from all their towns and villages to the temple in Jerusalem for the annual feasts. The road was often long and difficult, and there were dangers of inclement weather, wild animals, and bandits along the way. Consequently, during this journey, it was customary for the travelers to sing a "song of ascent" – one of fourteen psalms specially designed for these travelers. Our psalm today is one of these "songs of ascent", and in our passage we will learn some valuable things about God's watchful care over us.

Read: _Psalm 121_

"I will lift up my eyes to the mountains; From where shall my help come? 2 My help comes from the Lord, Who made heaven and earth. 3 He will not allow your foot to slip; He who keeps you will not slumber. 4 Behold, He who keeps Israel Will neither slumber nor sleep. 5 The Lord is your keeper; The Lord is your shade on your right hand."

*"6 The sun will not smite you by day, Nor the moon by night.
7 The Lord will [a]protect you from all evil; He will keep your soul. 8 The Lord will
[b] guard your going out and your coming in from this time forth and forever."*
(NIV)

Big Idea: God's watchful care is reliable, tailor-made, and motivated by His love for us.

1a. What Do You Think of When You Hear the Words "Dependence" or "Depend On"? _____
_____
_____
_____

For the journey the psalmist is about to embark on, his dependence on God is clear to see in verses 1-2: *"I lift my eyes up to the mountain – where does my help come from? My help comes from the LORD, the Maker of heaven and earth."* Notice that the Psalmist doesn't depend on his own knowledge as his source of strength; he doesn't turn to money or place his trust in a government official. The writer is confident and convinced that his help comes from the Living God, the *"...Maker of heaven and earth."*

2. For what reasons is depending on God worthwhile?

    a. _____
    b. _____
    c. _____
    d. _____

From our passage, we see three reasons for the psalmist's confidence in God. For one, the Psalmist knows that God's assistance is reliable, as we see in verse 3: *"He will not let your foot slip; he who watches over you will not slumber..."* This is a great image, when you think about it, because people get tired and run down, and our bodies are made to need rest. But God is not limited by these restrictions. He never grows tired or weary (Isaiah 40:28-31); His care is reliable and never lacking!

3. **What Do the Following Verses Say About God's Reliability:**

Deuteronomy 31:8	
Psalm 20:6-9	
Psalm 55:16-18	
2 Thessalonians 3:3	
Hebrews 13:8	

4. **What Does It Look Like for a Person to Place Their Confidence in God?** *(Explain your Answer)* _____

_____

_____

_____

The Psalmist also recognizes that God's care is tailor-made. In verse 5, the Psalmist makes the distinction that, *"The LORD watches over you..."* Implying that God's care is specific to us and our lives.

5. **In What Areas Do I Need God's Special Tailor-Made Help in My Life?** *(Explain Your Answers)*

_____

_____

_____

Insight: When God is watching over a person, He will provide exactly what is needed in life, because nothing is hidden from His sight. He knows every detail of our lives; therefore, we can trust His watchful care.

Then, finally, the writer trusts God's care because it is motivated by love. Look again at v. 8: *"The LORD will watch over your coming and going both now and forevermore."*

God's love never weakens or fades, and it will watch over us forever.

"God's care for us is more watchful and more tender than any human father could possibly be...and nothing can change His love for you." Author Unknown

7.   What Do the Following Verses Show About God's Loving Care?

Psalm 32:6-8	
Matthew 11:28-30	
Romans 8:38-39	
1 Peter 5:7	

Many people turn to many different things for strength and comfort in life. Some are valid and make sense, and some don't. But we, as children of God, have the best place to turn when life gets hard or we find ourselves in a confusing situation. The God of the universe intimately cares for and has His eye on us.

Challenge
To what or whom do I tend to turn when I need assistance? _____ _____ _____ *Do I come to God first and foremost, or is He my last resort?* _____ _____ _____ *How can I learn to trust God's care in my life?* _____ _____ _____

Going Deeper:

Many believe this Psalm was written by King Hezekiah, the 13th ruler of the southern kingdom of Judah in the Old Testament. Throughout his reign, Hezekiah was responsible for nationwide spiritual reform, because they had become a people who had grown apathetic toward the things of God. Hezekiah's leadership sparked national revival, as the people reopened the doors to the Temple and put aside their idols. Hezekiah was said to have a close relationship with God, which I think is evident because you can tell that he relied fully on God for help – just like we should!

The **Bible Knowledge Commentary** also says this about songs of ascent: *"The title 'song of ascent' identifies each of Psalms 120-134 as a pilgrim song to be sung when the Israelites 'ascended' (went up) to Jerusalem for the annual feasts. Four of these 15 psalms are ascribed to David (Ps. 122; 124; 131; 133), 1 to Solomon (Ps. 127), and the other ten are anonymous...The pilgrim-psalmist [in Psalm 121], as he contemplated his journey through the hills to Jerusalem, asked where his help came from. He found the answer to his question in the affirmation of his faith that the LORD, who created heaven and earth – with those hills – was his only Source of help,"* **1**

Going Deeper Response
USE A BIBLE COMMENTARY AND LOOK UP THE PSALM 121.

Pray: Asking God to help me trust the help He provides and not rely on my own understanding or strength...

_____

Lesson written by Pastor Frank & Samuel Gervasi

_____

Works Cited:

1. Walvoord, John F. and Zuck, Roy B. "Psalm 120-A Contemplation of the Journey", from *The Bible Knowledge Commentary*, SP Publications, Inc., 1985, pg. 882-883.
2. New International Bible, Holy Bible, New International Version®, NIV® Copyright ©1973, 1978, 1984, 2011 by Biblica, Inc.® Used by permission. All rights reserved worldwide.

Lesson 9 – "Grace in Action"

Memory Verse: *"When they persisted in asking him, he straightened up and said to them, 'He who is without sin among you, let him be the first to throw a stone at her.'"* **John 8:7, NIV**

Open in Prayer:

Introduction:

I heard a story once about a pastor who, one Sunday morning, found the roads to his church blocked. Due to this unexpected obstacle, he was forced to skate on the river to get there. When he arrived, the elders of the church were horrified to learn that their preacher had skated on Sunday – the Lord's Day!. After the service they held a meeting where the pastor explained that it was either skate to church or not go at all. After a pause, one elder asked, "Did you enjoy it?" When the preacher answered, "No," the board cleared him of wrongdoing. 1

Read *John 8:1-11*

"But Jesus went to the Mount of Olives. 2 At dawn he appeared again in the temple courts, where all the people gathered around him, and he sat down to teach them. 3 The teachers of the law and the Pharisees brought in a woman caught in adultery. They made her stand before the group 4 and said to Jesus, "Teacher, this woman was caught in the act of adultery. 5 In the Law Moses commanded us to stone such women. Now what do you say?" 6 They were using this question as a trap, in order to have a basis for accusing him. But Jesus bent down and started to write on the ground with his finger."

7 When they kept on questioning him, he straightened up and said to them, "Let any one of you who is without sin be the first to throw a stone at her." 8 Again he stooped down and wrote on the ground. 9 At this, those who heard began to go away one at a time, the older ones first, until only Jesus was left, with the woman still standing there. 10 Jesus straightened up and asked her, "Woman, where are they? Has no one condemned you?" 11 "No one, sir," she said. "Then neither do I condemn you," Jesus declared. "Go now and leave your life of sin."
(NIV)

<u>Big Idea:</u> *Grace looks beyond the letter of the law to a person's heart, bringing forgiveness, restoration, conviction, and change.*

In our passage today, we find a similarly legalistic group of Pharisees bringing before Jesus a woman caught in adultery. From verse 6, we learn that, *"They were using this question to trap him..." and* make Him say something that would discredit His reputation. Instead, Christ responded with wisdom, and modeled to us the mindset we should have when it comes to grace.

1. **Why Can Showing Grace Come hard sometimes?** *(Explain Your Answer)* _____
   _____
   _____
   _____
   _____

2. **What Do the Following Verses Say About the Law?**

Deuteronomy 4:5-6	
Deuteronomy 5:1	
Deuteronomy 6:24-25	
Deuteronomy 7:11-13	
Deuteronomy 8:11	

The adulterous woman's accusers were *"the teachers of the law and the Pharisees"* (v. 2), both of which went to great lengths to follow Mosaic Law. In fact, these religious leaders were correct in what Mosaic Law prescribed regarding the punishment for adultery (v. 5). However, they completely threw mercy and compassion out the window in the process, and their real intentions behind this episode were dishonest and self-serving.

But whereas the religious leaders condemned the woman for her failure, Jesus responds with grace: *"When they persisted in asking him, he straightened up and said to them, 'He who is without sin among you, let him be the first to throw a stone at her.'"* (v. 7)

Insight: *Grace not only pardons and forgives us but causes us to pursue holy living. When we understand the power of grace, we don't want to abuse it in any way. Grace should always produce change and lead us to something better.*

3. **Rate Yourself in Showing Compassion. 1 (Lowest) – 10 (Highest).**

1 _____ 2 _____ 3 _____ 4 _____ 5 _____ 6 _____ 7 _____ 8 _____ 9 _____ 10 _____

4. **What Areas Do You Find it Hardest to Show in Compassion in?** *(Why. Explain)*
   a. _____ b. _____
   c. _____ d. _____

He didn't have to do a lot, did He? Jesus' question itself brought conviction to the religious leaders and caused them to evaluate their own lives. And in response, *"...they began leaving one by one..."* (v. 9), for none present could claim that they had never sinned.

5. What Do the Following Verses Show About God's Grace?

Zech. 2:10-11	
John 1:16-17	
Acts 11:23-24	
Acts 14:3	
2 Corinthians 12:9	

In the end, only Jesus and the woman remained. Notice how he didn't yell at her or attack her. He didn't ask, "What's wrong with you? I can't believe you fell again!" Instead, *"...Jesus said, 'I do not condemn you either. Go. From now on, do not sin any longer.'"* (v. 11) Some versions translate it as, *"'Then neither do I condemn you. Go now and leave your life of sin.'"* It was the grace that was shown that day that probably changed that woman forever!

The same is true for us. It is ultimately the grace that God has shown to us that acquits us of our wrongdoings, forgives us, empowers us, and prompts us to change. And because it was freely shown to us, we should show it to others as well! I heard one person say it like this:

"The people who tend to be the most gracious are those who know how badly they need grace." Unknown

---

Challenge:

HOW MIGHT I SEE THE POWER OF GRACE THAT CAUSES CHANGE IN MY OWN LIFE?
_____
_____
_____

HOW CAN I GROW IN GRACE? _____
_____
_____

HOW CAN I SHOW GRACE TO OTHERS? _____
_____
_____
_____
_____

Going Deeper:

Warren Wiersbe once said this: *"We must not misinterpret this event to mean that Jesus was easy on sin or that He contradicted the law. For Jesus to forgive this woman meant that He had to one day die for her sins. Forgiveness is free, but it is not cheap. Furthermore, Jesus perfectly fulfilled the law so that no one could justly accuse Him of opposing its teachings or weakening its power....The law was given to reveal sin (Rom. 3:20), and we must be condemned by the law before we can be cleansed by God's grace. Law and grace do not compete; they complement each other. Nobody was ever saved by keeping the law, but nobody was ever saved by grace who was not first indicted by the law. There must be conviction before there can be conversion." 2*

Going Deeper Response

FIND A BIBLE CONCORDANCE AND LOOK UP GRACE. WRITE DOWN HOW MANY ARE CONCERNING PEOPLE SHOWING GRACE. AND HOW MANY CONCERN GOD SHOWING GRACE: GOD: _____
PEOPLE: _____

Close in Prayer Asking God to Show You How to Extend Grace to Others.....

Lesson written by Pastor Frank & Samuel Gervasi

Works Cited:

1. Today in the Word, Moody Publishers, December 1989, p. 12
2. Warren Wiersbe, Copyright © Warren W. Wiersbe.

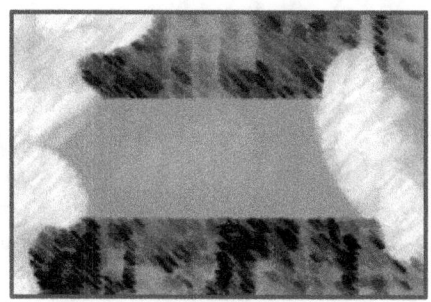

Lesson 10 – Learning to Speak Wisely?

Memory Verse: *"For if we could control our tongues, we would be perfect and could also control ourselves in every other way."*
James 3:2b, NIV

Open in Prayer:

Introduction:

A husband and wife tell a story about how recently they *"sat down to eat in a local restaurant."* And the husband, *"had gone to the restroom and when the server came over to get our drink orders, my wife said, 'We'll both have water, and I'll have iced tea. I don't know what he'll drink.' The server responded, 'So what's he going to do with the water?'"* 1

Our words are powerful and can be used in a positive but also negative way causing harm if not careful. In our passage today, in the book of James. It's one where he compares our speech with three different things, a fire, a ship, and a horse. And each one has something in common, a small thing having a big effect.

Read: **James 3:1-12**

"Not many of you should become teachers, my fellow believers, because you know that we who teach will be judged more strictly. 2 We all stumble in many ways. Anyone who is never at fault in what they say is perfect, able to keep their whole body in check. 3 When we put bits into the mouths of horses to make them obey us, we can turn the whole animal. 4 Or take ships as an example. Although they are so large and are driven by strong winds, they are steered by a

*very small rudder wherever the pilot wants to go. 5 Likewise, the tongue is a small part of the body, but it makes great boasts. Consider what a great forest is set on fire by a small spark. 6 The tongue also is a fire, a world of evil among the parts of the body. It corrupts the whole body, sets the whole course of one's life on fire, and is itself set on fire by hell. 7 All kinds of animals, birds, reptiles and sea creatures are being tamed and have been tamed by mankind, 8 but no human being can tame the tongue. It is a restless evil, full of deadly poison. 9 With the tongue we praise our Lord and Father, and with it we curse human beings, who have been made in God's likeness. 10 Out of the same mouth come praise and cursing. My brothers and sisters, this should not be. 11 Can both fresh water and saltwater flow from the same spring? 12 My brothers and sisters, can a fig tree bear olives, or a grapevine bear figs? Neither can a salt spring produce fresh water." **(NIV)***

Big Idea: *Our Speech is Powerful! –So, We Should Use Caution When We Speak.*

Even though our tongues are a small part of our bodies, our words can have big effects, can't they? And we can use them for good, or we can allow them to destroy and hurt other people. We saw in verse 5: *"Even so the tongue is a little member and boasts great things."* Even though James uses the word tongue he's obviously referring to our speech, the words we say and the things that come out of our mouths. What comes out of our mouths when we interact with those around us, ---matters to God.

1. **Why Should Our Speech Matter?** (*Explain Your Answer*) _____
    _____
    _____
    _____

    2. Have You Ever Been Hurt by Someone Because of What They Said?
    (Explain How You Felt?) _____
    _____
    _____
    _____

James describes our tongue as something small but powerful in verse 5b-6: *"A small thing that makes grand speeches. But a tiny spark can set a great forest on fire."* I think it's an excellent picture when he's talking about our speech. Because some of the World's largest and most destructive forest fires all started with one spark.

3. Look Up the Following Verses and Write What Stands Out?

Job 15:3-6	
Psalm 19:2-4	
Proverbs 8:13	
Ecc. 5:5-6	
Acts 5:40-42	

Insight: *Even Though it's Difficult Our Speech Should Be Mastered - So We Can Live Wisely!*

Nevertheless, even though it's difficult we can't use it as an excuse because God still wants us to use our speech in a way that honors Him. So, we need to learn to discipline our speech, regardless of the difficulty.

4. Why Do You Think Speech Be Difficult for People? (Explain Your Answer) _____

_____
_____
_____
_____

5. What Times Are Speech Difficult to Control for You? (Explain Your Answer) _____

_____
_____

If we look starting in v. 7, James likens our speech with all the various animals that have been tamed by man. However, our speech being very difficult to master. *"For every species of beasts and birds, of reptiles and creatures of the sea, is tamed and has been tamed by the human race. But no one can tame the tongue; it is a restless evil and full of deadly poison."*

6. *Look Up the Following Scripture and Write What Stands Out About Our Words?*_

2 Cor. 8:7	
1 Timothy 4:12	
Titus 2:7-9	
1 Peter 3:9-10	

God cares about how we use our speech, and our words should be controlled because they are powerful. So, we should learn to use our speech in ways that build others up and encourage them.

I heard one person say: *"you can tell a person's character by the words he or she uses!"* (unknown)

Challenge:

HOW MIGHT I USE MY SPEECH TO BUILD OTHERS UP AND NOT TEAR DOWN?

_____

_____

_____

HOW CAN I SPEAK IN AN EDIFYING WAY? _____

_____

_____

WHO DO I NEED TO APPOLOGIZE TO FOR MY SPEECH? _____

_____

_____

Going Deeper:

The term here _"perfect"_ in verse 2 is not referring to absence of fault. However, it is speaking of the _"spiritual maturity"_ that Christians should be striving for. The **NIV Study Bible Notes** also confirms and expands on this important word by saying that if a person could tame their tongue, it would most likely filter over into other areas of their life as well. _"Since the tongue is so difficult to control, those who control it perfectly gain control of themselves in all other areas of life as well. James indicates that complete control of the tongue, if it were possible, would render a person 'perfect.' This reflects the same Greek term from 1:4, where it indicates 'maturity.'"_

Even though it is difficult, we should learn to master our speech in a way that helps and _not_ hurts others. **Ephesians 4:29** is the standard that was set by the apostle Paul as well when he says: _"Let no [a]unwholesome word proceed from your mouth, but only such a word as is good for edification [b]according to the need of the moment, so that it will give grace to those who hear."_ **2**

Going Deeper Response
CFHOOSE A PERSON YOU CAN CALL AND ENCOURAGE THIS WEEK AND INVITE TO CHURCH AND A CUP OF COFFEE

<u>Pray:</u> **Thanking God for the ability to use my speech in a good way. Asking for the power I need to master it....**

———————————

Lesson written by Pastor Frank & Samuel Gervasi

———————————————

<u>Works Cited:</u>

1. Speaker Stories, https://speakerstories.wordpress.com/2012/04/16/people-are-funny/, as accessed on 03/20/2025.
2. NIV Study Bible, Copyright © 1985, 1995, 2002, 2008, 2011 by Zondervan.

Lesson 11 Confidence in God

Memory Verse: *"But joyful are those who have the God of Israel as their helper, whose hope is in the Lord their God."*
Psalm 146:5, NIV

Open in Prayer:

Introduction:

There is a story about a father who went rock climbing with his son, Zac. The two were out in the country, climbing around in some cliffs, when the father heard a voice from above him yell, "Hey Dad! Catch me!" He turned around to see Zac joyfully jumping off a rock straight toward him. He had jumped first and then yelled "Hey Dad!" Things became an instant circus act, as the father moved into position to catch him. Both fell to the ground. When the father found his voice again, he gasped in exasperation: "Zac! Can you give me one good reason why you did that???" He responded with remarkable calmness: "Sure...because you're my dad." [1]

We all place our trust in someone or something. Many times, we choose to trust other people, expecting them to be looking out for us. In some situations, that trust is well-placed, like with Zac and his dad. But other times we place our confidence in the wrong people for the wrong things. As we'll see in our devotion today, there is only one Person in whom we should be placing our ultimate confidence. And we should be overflowing with thankfulness when we realize just how reliable He is.

Read: Psalm 146

"Praise the Lord. [a] Praise the Lord, my soul. 2 I will praise the Lord all my life; I will sing praise to my God as long as I live. 3 Do not put your trust in princes, in human beings, who cannot save. 4 When their spirit departs, they return to the ground; on that very day their plans come to nothing. 5 Blessed are those whose help is the God of Jacob, whose hope is in the Lord their God. 6 He is the Maker of heaven and earth, the sea, and everything in them— he remains faithful forever. 7 He upholds the cause of the oppressed and gives food to the hungry. The Lord sets prisoners free, 8 the Lord gives sight to the blind, the Lord lifts up those who are bowed down, the Lord loves the righteous. 9 The Lord watches over the foreigner and sustains the fatherless and the widow, but he frustrates the ways of the wicked. 10 The Lord reigns forever, your God, O Zion, for all generations. Praise the Lord." (NIV)

Big Idea: *We should never place our confidence in people but rather give our trust and worship to God.*

Last week, we saw how Psalm 146 exhorts us to worship joyfully before God, and in these verses, we now see one of the reasons we should give God that praise: people fail, but God does not. Look at vv. 3-4: *"Don't put your confidence in powerful people; there is no help for you there. When they breathe their last, they return to the earth, and all their plans die with them."*

1. **Describe the Difference Between Worship & Praise?** *(Be Specific)* ____
   _____
   _____
   _____

2. **What Are Common Things People Place Their Confidence in?** (Expand on Your Answers) _____
   _____
   _____
   _____

We can see something clearly in these verses: God may be worthy of our adoration, but people will never measure up in the same ways. And that will be true of even the best, wisest, most respectable person we could know. They will still always be lacking, because they will always be limited to what extent they can help us.

3. Look Up the Following Verses and Discover What They Say About God?

1 Chronicles 16:25-27	
Psalm 18:3-6	
Psalm 96:3-5	
Matthew 3:11	

3. What Are Reasons God is Worthy of Our Praise? (Be Specific)

a. _____ b. _____

c. _____ d. _____

Verse 3 describes *"powerful people"* or some versions say *"princes"*. We can all picture someone who fits this description – someone with influence and status. Nevertheless, even these people will let us down at one point or another.

But isn't it good news to know that God will never let us down? Look at the contrast between vv. 3-4 (which we read earlier) and vv. 5-6: *"But joyful are those who have the God of Israel as their helper, whose hope is in the LORD their God. He made heaven and earth, the sea, and everything in them. He keeps every promise forever."*

4. How Do the Following Verses Describe God?

Deuteronomy 33:29	
Psalm 10:14-18	
Psalm 27:9-10	
Hebrews 13:6	

Even the most trustworthy people on earth will fall short and fail us, but we serve the never-failing God of Armies. How should we respond? The psalmist responds in jubilant praise! Throughout the rest of the psalm, he demonstrates his thankfulness and gratitude for the faithfulness and reliability of his King. Let's offer our trust and affection to God as well and choose to place our confidence in Him rather than fallible human beings. And let's worship joyfully before the Lord!

Insight: *Trust and praise have a symbiotic relationship. When we choose to place our confidence in God, we are moved to worship Him. Likewise, when we worship God even in the harshest trials, we find it easier to have faith in God's perfect plan.*

---

5. ***What Things Do I Have to Be Grateful to God for***? (Explain Your Answers)

   a. _____

   b. _____

   c. _____

   d. _____

Challenge:
WHERE HAVE I BEEN PLACING MY CONFIDENCE? _____ _____ _____
WHAT DO I NEED TO TRUST GOD WITH TODAY? _____ _____ _____
WHY HAVENT I TRUSTED HIM IN THESE AREAS? _____ _____ _____

Going Deeper:

Matthew Henry, in his Commentary on the Whole Bible, says regarding verses 3-4: *"David is supposed to have penned this psalm; and he was himself a prince, a mighty prince; as such, it might be thought...that he himself, having been so great a blessing to his country, should be adored, according to the usage of the heathen nations, who deified their heroes, that they should all come and trust in his shadow and make him their stay and strong-hold. 'No,' says David, 'Put not your trust in princes (Ps. 146:3), not in me, not in any other; do not repose your confidence in them; do not raise your expectations from them. Be not too sure of their sincerity; some thought they knew better how to reign by knowing how to dissemble. Be not too sure of their constancy and fidelity; it is possible they may both change their minds and break their words.' But though we suppose them very wise and as good as David himself, yet we must not be too sure of their ability and continuance, for they are sons of Adam, weak and mortal. There is indeed a Son of man in whom there is help, in whom there is salvation, and who will not fail those that trust in him."* **2**

Going Deeper Response
MAKE A GRATITUDE LIST ABOUT THE TANGIBLE WAYS GOD HAS PROVIDED AND HELPED YOU THIS PAST YEAR.

Pray Thanking God for All the Ways He Helped you in Life.....

———————————

Lesson written by Pastor Frank & Samuel Gervasi

———————————

1. Adapted from https://www.sermonillustrations.com/a-z/t/trust.htm; as accessed on 11/20/2024
2. Matthew Henry's Commentary on the Whole Bible, public domain.

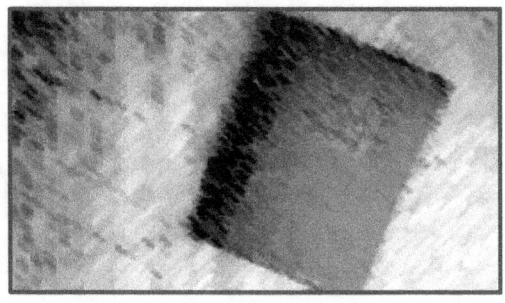

Lesson 12 - God's Useful Book

Memory Verse: *"All Scripture is God-breathed and is useful for teaching, rebuking, correcting and training in righteousness, 17 so that the servant of God may be thoroughly equipped for every good work."* 2 Timothy 3:16-17, NIV

Open in Prayer:

Read: *2 Timothy 3:14-17*

Introduction:

"A Roman Catholic priest in Belgium rebuked a young woman and her brother for reading that 'bad book' pointing to the Bible. 'Mr. Priest,' she replied, 'a little while ago my brother was an idler, a gambler, a drunkard, and made such a noise in the house that no one could stay in it. Since he began to read the Bible, he works with industry, goes no longer to the tavern, no longer touches cards, brings home money to his poor old mother, and our life at home is quiet and delightful. How comes it, Mr. Priest, that a bad book produces such good fruits?'" 1

"But as for you, continue in what you have learned and have become convinced of, because you know those from whom you learned it, 15 and how from infancy you have known the Holy Scriptures, which are able to make you wise for salvation through faith in Christ Jesus. 16 All Scripture is God-breathed and is useful for teaching, rebuking, correcting and training in righteousness, 17 so that the servant of God[a] may be thoroughly equipped for every good work." **(NIV)**

Big Idea: *The Bible Came from God's mouth, through the individual writers affirming its useability....*

The Bible is transformative and can change people for the good.

In fact, it has been said by some to be a divinely fortified book-not just any book- so it can be believed fully. That is probably true for several reasons however, because it's not just some great literary work, like we might see in a university, or a library, or even in a bookstore. We can place our trust in its reliability because it's more of a literary miracle, if anything. There really can't be anything earthly compared with it, because it's not earthly in its origin.

Consider, that a group of individuals didn't sit on a committee and even plan the sixty-six books of the Bible. Rather, more than forty different authors labored for over a span of sixty generations and over three continents. We saw in v. 16 that: *"All Scripture is God-breathed."* Carrying this idea that it came directly from God's mouth and speaking through everyday people of various backgrounds.

1. ***What Are Reasons People Might Not Believe the Bible's Reliability?***
   (Explain) _____
   _____
   _____
   _____
   _____

2. ***What Practical Areas of Life Can the Bible Be Applied?*** (Be Specific)
   a. _____ *b.* _____
   c. _____ *d.* _____

3. **Read the Following Verses and Describe What is Affected by the Scriptures?**

Daniel 9:2	
Psalm 119:1-6	
Matthew 22:29	
Luke 24:27	
Acts 17:11-12	
Romans 15:4	

<u>Insight:</u> *The Bible is Useful for Training in Righteousness -That We May Be Equipped!*

The Bible is also an especially *pertinent* book with uses that lead to spiritual growth because it's not a book that is just useful for something trivial, or something just to pass the time. It's a book that has a clear, decisive and important function, that's relevant for all things. However, it's especially useful for the matter in the spiritual growth of anyone.

In v.16 it says: *"All Scripture, is God-breathed and is useful for teaching, rebuking, correcting and training in righteousness."*

4. **What Three Aspects of Spiritual Growth is the Bible Pertinent For?**

a. _____ b. _____

c. _____ d. _____

e. _____ f. _____

5. *Explain the Difference Between Reading Your Bible and Studying Your Bible?* (Explain Your Answers) _____
_____
_____
_____
_____

He lists clear benefits or uses that come from God's word that even though he was telling Timothy about, are for really everyone, regardless of who we are. One version uses the word *"profitable"* which I kind of like, because it's kind of just gets your attention more than *useful*. That we can profit when we read the bible is encouraging to say the least. He also expands in v. 16 when he says: *"Teaching, rebuking, correcting."* All things that are needed at different seasons of a Christ follower's life in many cases.

6. *What is the Benefit of God's Word in the Following Verses?*

Leviticus 25:18	
Joshua 1:7-8	
Acts 18:28	
1 Corinthians 15:3-4	

Finally, we don't read the Bible not to acquire information or be puffed up with knowledge but that we grow in faith, holiness, and purity. In the last part of v. 16 the Apostle Paul was giving Timothy the final goal of the Bible, *"and training in righteousness."*

God's ultimate desire for his children is that we all grow in righteousness and apply what we learn. There is probably no book that's more relevant for today's culture, even though it may look different than the culture of the day.

Nobody ever outgrows Scripture; the book widens and deepens with our years. –
Charles Spurgeon 2

Challenge:
HOW CAN I DO GOOD TO THOSE AROUND ME? _____   _____   _____   _____   WHAT AREA OF THE BIBLE DO I NEED TO GROW IN? _____   _____   _____   _____   WHAT AREAS HAVE I NOT ALLOWED THE BIBLE TO NOT CHANGE ME? _____   _____   _____   _____   _____

Going Deeper:

Context might clarify the times that were prevalent during the writing of first and second Timothy. There were a lot of different works that were popular, however, written works were not as readily available as today. However, both Jews and Christians were relying heavily on Old Testament Scrolls and the new letters and epistles that were being circulated among the churches. In fact, **Zondervan Illustrated Bible Backgrounds Commentary of the New Testament** says:

"The religions of Greece and Rome in Paul's time were not dependent on written materials. There were sacred books containing oracular materials (e.g., the Sibylline Oracles), magic books with spells, incantations, charms, and so forth (cf. Acts 19:19),

and other kinds of handbooks on practices such as augury (the interpretation of various omens). Moreover, the writing of the ancient poets like Homer or Hesiod were regarded as having particular authority in their myths about the gods, though at the same time there was a popular saying: 'The poets tell many lies,' especially about the gods. In contrast, both Judaism and its offspring, Christianity, were and are religions that rely heavily on the inspired and authoritative Scriptures." **3**

Going Deeper Response

MAKE A PRAYER LIST ABOUT THE TANGIBLE WAYS YOU NEED GOD'S HELP FOR AND COMMIT TO READ YOUR BIBLE 3 SPECIFIC TIMES THIS WEEK

<u>**Pray:**</u> *Asking God for the desire and wisdom to learn the Scriptures in a greater way and apply them....*

_____

Lesson written by Pastor Frank & Samuel Gervasi

_____

Works Cited:

1. Ministry 127, https://ministry127.com/resources/illustration/the-fruit-of-the-bible/ as accessed on 09/15/2024
2. Deeper Christian Quotes, https://deeperchristian.com/scripture-study-quotes/, as accessed on 04/12/2025.
3. (Zondervan Illustrated Bible Backgrounds Commentary of the New Testament, Copyright © 2002. All rights reserved.

Lesson 13 – Follow Me

Memory Verse: *"And whoever does not carry their cross and follow me cannot be my disciple."* **Luke 14:27, NIV**

Open in Prayer:

Introduction:

Phillip "Jim" Eliot was an evangelist and Christian missionary who died pursuing his life's ambition of taking the gospel to unreached people. On January 8, 1956, he and four American missionary companions were speared to death on a remote beach by ten men of the primitive Auca/Waorani tribe—the tribe he had felt called to evangelize. Yet Jim Eliot's widow, Elisabeth, held no grudges toward her husband's murderers. Instead, she and several other women moved to the Auca village to continue the work their husbands began. Just one year after the five missionaries were slain in Ecuador, she wrote, "We have proved beyond any doubt that [God] means what He says – His grace is sufficient, nothing can separate us from the love of Christ. We pray that if any, anywhere, are fearing that the cost of discipleship is too great, that they may be given to glimpse that treasure in heaven promised to all who forsake." 1

Read: *Luke 14:25-35*

"Large crowds were traveling with Jesus and turning to them he said: 26 "If anyone comes to me and does not hate father and mother, wife and children, brothers and sisters—yes, even their own life—such a person cannot be my disciple. 27 And whoever does not carry their cross and follow me cannot be my disciple. 28 "Suppose one of you wants to build a tower. Won't you first sit down and estimate the cost to see if you have enough money to complete it? 29 For if you lay the foundation and are not able to finish it, everyone who sees it will ridicule you,"

"30 saying, 'This person began to build and wasn't able to finish.' 31 "Or suppose a king is about to go to war against another king. Won't he first sit down and consider whether he is able with ten thousand men to oppose the one coming against him with twenty thousand? 32 If he is not able, he will send a delegation while the other is still a long way off and will ask for terms of peace. 33 In the same way, those of you who do not give up everything you have cannot be my disciples. 34 "Salt is good, but if it loses its saltiness, how can it be made salty again? 35 It is fit neither for the soil nor for the manure pile; it is thrown out. 'Whoever has ears to hear, let them hear.'" (NIV)

Big Idea: *Jesus wants every part of our lives, both spiritual and physical, devoted to Him and His kingdom.*

Sometimes the Christian life can demand a lot from the believer. In a spiritual sense, following Jesus can always seem to stretch a person, because everybody brings a different background, character flaws, and ways of doing things that God wants to alter. Even physically, believers may experience sickness and disease that God uses for His glory.

1. **What Habits or Mindsets Do You Feel That You Brought into Your Christian Life?** _____
_____
_____
_____

2. **What Area Has Been the Hardest to Let Go of or Leave Behind?**

a. _____ b. _____
c. _____ d. _____

In our passage today, we can clearly see that Jesus wants first place in our lives for all things. He wants our full allegiance, and the deepest place in our hearts.

We see in verse 26: *"If anyone comes to me and does not hate father and mother, wife and children…even their own life – such a person **cannot** be my disciple."* (emphasis added)

3. What Do the Following Verses Say About Being a Follower?

Leviticus 20:5-6	
Numbers 32:14-15	
Judges 2:19-21	
2 Kings 18:5-7	
Luke 9:57-62	
Philippians 3:17	

To clarify, Jesus is not saying that people should despise their families looking back in Luke; families are a gift from God (Matthew 15:4; 1 Timothy 5:8).

Rather, Jesus is saying we should be so thoroughly and passionately dedicated to Him, that our love for other things pales in comparison so much, it's like hatred. To be a disciple, you must love Jesus more than those relationships.

Insight: *We must understand our commitment in walking with Christ, so we aren't discouraged when life gets hard. Because following Jesus is the most important decision a person can make. God wants whole-hearted disciples that are committed to complete surrender.*

---

4. What Does Surrender Mean in Your Own Words? *(Be Specific)*

_____

_____

_____

_____

5. *What Stands Out in the Following Verses About Yielding?*

Joshua 24:23	
Psalm 85:12	
Isaiah 42:8	
1 Corinthians 7:2-4	

Sometimes, that wholehearted allegiance means dying to the old ways of life. Look at verse 27: *"Whoever does not carry their cross and follow me cannot be my disciple."* Think about that – Jesus wants our goals, our plans, and our dreams submitted completely for His use. To be identified with Christ means dying to old ways, old thought patterns, even old relationships if they hinder our walk with the Lord. Finally, look at verse 33: *"In the same way, those of you who do not give up everything you have **cannot be my disciples**."* It doesn't get much clearer than that! Our families, our careers, our desires, even the tangible things we take for granted, belong to God. And when we lay those things at His feet to follow Him, we'll find it was the best place to put them.

"Salvation is free, but discipleship will cost you your life." Dietrich Bonhoeffer 2

Challenge:

WHAT DOES IT COST ME TO FOLLOW JESUS? _____

_____

_____

WHAT DOES IT MEAN TO BE IDENTIFIED WITH CHRIST? _____

_____

_____

WHAT WAYS HAS FOLLOWING CHRIST MADE ME A BETTER PERSON? _____

_____

_____

Going Deeper:

Verse 34 says, *"Salt is good, but if it loses its saltiness, how can it be made salty again? It is fit neither for the soil nor for the manure pile; it is thrown out."* Regarding this verse, the John MacArthur Study Bible says this: *"Salt was an essential item in first-century Palestine...In a hot climate, without refrigeration, salt was the practical means of preserving food." 3* In the same way, we should leave others that we encounter wanting to know more about our faith.

Going Deeper Response
MAKE A LIST DETAILING THE AREAS WHERE WE FEEL WE NEED TO LEAVE OTHERS WANTING MORE OF CHRIST. THEN COMMIT THOSE AREAS IN PRAYER...

<u>Pray:</u>   *Close in Prayer for God to help me follow Him, no matter what it costs me*

Lesson written by Pastor Frank & Samuel Gervasi

Works Cited:

1. Christianity Today, Vol. 1, reprinted Vol. 40, no. 10, https://www.gotquestions.org/Jim-Elliot.html, as accessed on 03/20/2025
2. Dietrich Bonhoffer, The Cost of Discipleship, pg. 39, New York: Macmillan Publishing Company, 1963; first published, 1937.
3. MacArthur Study Bible, Bible Gateway Plus, www.biblrgateway.com, Copyright © John F. MacArthur, published by Thomas Nelson, 2006.

Lesson: 14 – Doing Your Best

Memory Verse: *"Let us not become weary in doing good, for at the proper time we will reap a harvest if we do not give up."* **Galatians 6:9, NIV**

Open In Prayer:

Introduction:

"It took less than ten seconds for Jamaican sprinter Usain Bolt to cover the one-hundred-meter distance on the Olympic track and win the gold medal in London. Those few seconds cemented his status as the "fastest man alive" and placed him on the winner's podium once again. But the race was not won in those seconds—it was won by hours and hours of practice, workouts, weightlifting, special diet, and coaching. The race was not won in the performance but in the preparation. It is our desire for something greater that causes us to sacrifice some things, even some good things, for the sake of things that are better."[1]

Read Galatians 6:1-10

"Brothers and sisters, if someone is caught in a sin, you who live by the Spirit should restore that person gently. But watch yourselves, or you also may be tempted. 2 Carry each other's burdens, and in this way you will fulfill the law of Christ. 3 If anyone thinks they are something when they are not, they deceive themselves. 4 Each one should test their own actions. Then they can take pride in themselves alone, without comparing themselves to someone else, 5 for each one should carry their own load. 6 Nevertheless, the one who receives instruction in the word should share all good things with their instructor."

"Do not be deceived: God cannot be mocked. A man reaps what he sows. 8 Whoever sows to please their flesh, from the flesh will reap destruction; whoever sows to please the Spirit, from the Spirit will reap eternal life. 9 Let us not become weary in doing good, for at the proper time we will reap a harvest if we do not give up. 10 Therefore, as we have opportunity, let us do good to all people, especially to those who belong to the family of believers." **(NIV)**

Big Idea: *Doing Our Best is God's Will and Will Pay off in the Long Run.*

We may not make the same sacrifices an athlete makes, but we all must lay down a natural human tendency of complacency and pride, and choose to do our best, especially in matters of our faith. The Apostle Paul admonishes us in verse 4 to *"do good to everyone"*, and to *"share each other's burdens, and in this way obey the law of Christ."* V. 2.

These verses aren't saying that believers should follow *Mosaic* Law; rather, he was speaking in a fashion that some in that church understood. Although we are no longer under the Law, it's clear that doing good and living like Jesus *(the "law of Christ")* is pleasing to the Lord.

1. ***What Are Ways We Can Please Christ in Addition to Doing Good to Others?*** *(Explain our Answers)* _____
   _____
   _____
   _____

2. ***What Areas Have I Not Been Pleasing to Christ?*** *(Be Specific)* _____
   _____
   _____
   _____

Doing good starts with looking at ourselves first.

We see in verses 4-5: *"Pay careful attention to your **own** work, for then you will get the satisfaction of a job well done, and then you won't need to compare yourself to anyone else."* (NIV) This is good advice for all of us, because something gets lost when our attention starts focusing on what others should be doing. Although it may be difficult, we need to focus on our walk with Christ if we want to do our best, understanding that *"You are not that important."* V. 3b

3. **What stands out in the Following Verses?**

Judges 21:22	
Luke 8:3	
Acts 9:36	
1 Timothy 5:10	
Philemon 1:13	

Finally, look back at verses 9-10: *"So, let us not become weary in doing what is good. At just the right time we will reap a harvest of blessings if we do not give up. Therefore, whenever we have the opportunity, we should do good to everyone, especially in the family of faith."* (NIV)

Doing our best will always pay off in due time. We may not see it right away. We may not see it next month, or even next year. But God has promised He will bless those who do their best, in whatever form that blessing He chooses.

4. What Are Reasons Doing Good to Others Can Be Hard at Times?
(Explain Your Answers) _____
_____
_____
_____

5. Tell About a Time When Someone Did Good to You? *(Be Specific)* _____
_____
_____
_____
_____

Looking back in Galatians, notice that these verses say, *"**we will** reap a harvest"*. This phrase sounds definitive in the fact that those who do good will be rewarded by God's own hand. But notice that that harvest only comes *"if we do not give up"*. Don't be discouraged if the waiting is getting long; giving our best to God and obeying the law of Christ will be worth it in the end. Stand strong and continue choosing to do good until your harvest comes.

<u>Insight:</u>   *We will reap what we sow in life. Although God often graciously gives us what we don't deserve, it is a natural law of God that the more a person lives to please their flesh, the more death and decay they experience. We cannot live however we want; we must choose to live according to God's Word if we want to do our best and receive our reward.*

6. *What Do the Following Verses Say About Endurance?*

Romans 15:4	
2 Corinthians 1:24	
Colossians 1:9-11	
1 Thessalonians 1:3-7	
2 Timothy 3:10-11	

Challenge:

IN WHAT WAYS CAN I DO GOOD TO THOSE AROUND ME? _____
_____
_____

HOW CAN I GROW IN DOING GOOD? _____
_____
_____

WHAT AREAS NEED IMPROVEMENT? _____
_____
_____
_____

Going Deeper:

Regarding the principle of reaping and sowing, the CSB *Tony Evans Study Bible* says this:

"God has established certain laws that govern the universe he has made. This is true in the physical world (e.g., the law of gravity). But it's true of the spiritual world as well. Paul articulates an important spiritual law or principle when he says, whatever a person sows he will also reap. A farmer harvests exactly what he plants. If he sows potatoes, he won't be looking to harvest green beans. Decide what you want to harvest spiritually and let that control what you decide to sow. This law is universal (it applies to all people everywhere) and inviolable (it proves true without fail). Don't kid yourself into believing that you can rebel against God without consequence." **2**

Going Deeper Response
THINK OF 3-4 PEOPLE YOU KNOW AND MAKE A LIST DETAILING THE WAYS YOU CAN DO GOOD TO THEM. THEN MAKE THE TIME TO ACT ON THEM.

Pray: **Asking for God to help me persevere until the harvest comes, giving my best to Him and following His will...**

Lesson written by Pastor Frank & Samuel Gervasi

Works Cited:

1. Ministry 127, https://ministry127.com/resources/illustration/the-fastest-man-alive, as accessed on 03/20/2025.
2. Tony Evans Study Bible, Copyright © 2017 by Holman Bible Publishers, Bible Gateway Plus, www.biblegateway.com, as accessed on 03/20/2025.

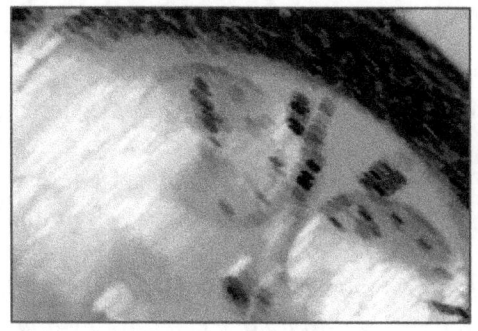

Lesson 15 – A Time for Everything

Memory Verse: *"There is a time for everything, and a season for every activity under the heavens..."* **Ecclesiastes 3:1, NIV**

Open in Prayer:

Introduction:

"If you're ever walking the streets of Boston and it starts to rain, look down—you might see something surprising. Boston's City Hall and the nonprofit group Mass Poetry are "slowly bringing secret art to the streets", through a combination of stencils, waterproof spray paint, and rainy days. Since the beginning of April, poems have been sprayed with waterproof paint on sidewalks throughout the city. When the sidewalk is dry, the words are invisible; but when the sidewalk is wet, a piece of art suddenly appears. For many people, a rainy day isn't an ideal day – but who knows what beautiful things a person might miss if it hadn't been for the rain?" 1

In life, seasons come, and seasons go. We cling tightly to some of them and refuse to move on to new ones. In others, we rush to move on as quickly as possible to a more comfortable situation. But we do not have very much say-so when they change. However, we do know that God has power over our seasons in life, regardless of how long they last.

Read: *Ecclesiastes 3:1-14*

"There is a time for everything, and a season for every activity under the heavens: 2 a time to be born and a time to die, a time to plant and a time to uproot, 3 a time to kill and a time to heal, a time to tear down and a time to build, 4 a time to weep and a time to laugh, a time to mourn and a time to dance, 5 a time to scatter

*stones and" a time to gather them, a time to embrace and a time to refrain from embracing, 6 a time to search and a time to give up, a time to keep and a time to throw away, 7 a time to tear and a time to mend, a time to be silent and a time to speak, 8 a time to love and a time to hate, a time for war and a time for peace. 9 What do workers gain from their toil? 10 I have seen the burden God has laid on the human race. 11 He has made everything beautiful in its time. He has also set eternity in the human heart; yet[a] no one can fathom what God has done from beginning to end. 12 I know that there is nothing better for people than to be happy and to do good while they live. 13 That each of them may eat and drink and find satisfaction in all their toil—this is the gift of God. 14 I know that everything God does will endure forever; nothing can be added to it and nothing taken from it. God does it so that people will fear him." **(NIV)***

Big Idea: *Every season in life, both good and bad, is sovereignly ordained by God and is needed to receive God's best for us.*

Notice how verse 1 says, *"There is a time for everything, and a season for every activity under the heavens..."* Some versions use the phrase *"appointed times"* (NASB), which implies that someone other than us is doing the appointing. And we know from the rest of Scripture that person is God Himself.

1. Why Can Thinking of Seasons Seem Comforting? *(Explain Your Answers)* _____
_____
_____
_____

2. How Can We Trust God During Difficult Seasons? *(Be Specific)* _____
_____
_____
_____
_____

Everything that happens to us can be traced back to God's sovereign hand. Absolutely nothing comes into our lives without either God being the originator, or without God allowing it. For some, this can be bad news. If a person is prideful and needs to take credit for the outcome or is uncomfortable trusting God without knowing why He allows the bad seasons, this passage is far from encouraging. But for those of us who choose submission and can rest in the promise that God will *"…cause all things to work together for the good of those who love him,"* (Romans 8:28, NIV) this passage is comforting to hear.

3. Look Up the Following Verses and Highlight What They Show About God's Sovereignty?

2 Samuel 7:20-22	
2 Samuel 7:28-29	
1 Kings 8:53	
Psalm 68:20	
Psalm 140:6-8	

Not only are all seasons, good and bad, ordained by God, but they are fully needed as well. Both highs and lows are important for every person; we cannot have one without the other. Verses 2-8 list *"A time for"* twenty-eight common events that many people go through in life. Most often, it's easier to welcome the good events identified in this list, and it's a lot easier to ignore or avoid the rough times. However, God uses both to accomplish His purposes in each person.

Insight: *Every season in life should cause us to fear God and develop a deep, healthy reverence for Him. Regardless of where we are in life, God is always worthy of our respect, honor, and reverence.*

---

4. What Common Events Are Going on in Your Life Where You See God's Hand Working? *(Explain Your Answers)*

a. _____ b. _____

c. _____ d. _____

5. If God has appointed every season of our lives, and is using them to accomplish His purposes in us, how are we to respond? *(Explain Your Answers)* _____

_____

_____

_____

We should learn to be content with whatever God has given us. Look again at verses 12-13: *"I know that there is nothing better for people than to be happy and to do good while they live. That each of them may eat and drink and find satisfaction in all their toil—this is the gift of God."* (NIV)

6. What Do the Following Verses Say About Contentment? *(Be Specific)*

Joshua 7:7	
Psalm 131:1-3	
Proverbs 19:23	
Luke 3:12-15	
1 Timothy 6:3-8	
Hebrews 13:5	

To clarify, I want to say that looking back in Ecclesiastes, these verses do not imply that we shouldn't aspire to better things in life. Or that we should accept everything that comes our way, even if others are treating us unfairly or unjustly. What it is saying is that we should learn to make the most of our everyday routines that we take for granted sometimes. Philippians 4:12-13 says this: *"I know what it is to be in need, and I know what it is to have plenty. I have learned the secret of being content in any and every situation, whether well fed or hungry, whether living in plenty or in want. I can do all this through him who gives me strength."* (NIV) We should be people who learn to be content with where God has us for that specific reason.

Challenge:

WHAT SEASON OF LIFE AM I IN RIGHT NOW? _____
_____
_____
_____

HOW CAN I LEARN TO FEAR GOD AND BE CONTENT WHERE I AM? _____
_____
_____
_____

WHAT HAS ME CONCERNED ABOUT THIS SEASON OF LIFE RIGHT NOW?
_____
_____
_____

Going Deeper:

Regarding Ecclesiastes 3, the *Jamieson, Fausset, & Brown Bible Commentary* says the following: *"Earthly pursuits are no doubt lawful in their proper time and order (Ecc 3:1-8), but unprofitable when out of time and place; as for instance, when pursued as the solid and chief good (Ecc 3:9, 10); whereas God makes everything beautiful in its season, which man obscurely comprehends (Ecc 3:11). God allows man to enjoy moderately and virtuously His earthly gifts (Ecc 3:12, 13). What consoles us amidst the instability of earthly blessings is, God's counsels are immutable (Ecc 3:14)." 2*

Going Deeper Challenge

LIST THE LAST 3 SEASONS YOU'VE HAD AND DESCRIBE IN DETAIL HOW GOD WORKED THEM OUT.

__Pray:__ Thanking God for both the good and tough times He has ordained and asking Him to help me be content....

_____

Lesson written by Pastor Frank & Samuel Gervasi

Works Cited:

1.   Preaching Today, https://www.preachingtoday.com/illustrations/2016/may/bostons-secret-street-art.html, as accessed on 03/20/2025.
2.   Jamieson, Fausset, & Brown Bible Commentary, 1971, Bible Gateway Plus, www.biblegateway.com, as accessed on 03/20/2025.

Going Deeper

Study Guide- Group Edition

Icebergs are pieces of ice that formed on land and float in a body of water. Consequently, it's said that 90% of an iceberg is below the water surface and unseen. When it comes to our beliefs and mindsets, they are also like an iceberg, not always on the surface. *The Going Deeper-Study Guide* was written to draw closer to God in committed time studying God's Word in a Small Group/Bible Study Format. Our hope is that wherever you are in your journey with God, that you will utilize the next 15-30 Lessons to draw closer to Him and uncover mindsets that hinder our lives. Our prayer is that as you use this daily time and study God's word in a deeper way, and that you will grow.

Frank Gervasi – Pastor Frank was raised in a Catholic home, to Italian parents, on Chicago's Southwest side.

In his early twenties was invited to an inner-city church, after a time of seeking God. While there he heard the Gospel preached with power for the first time and accepted the Lord on June 3, 1993.

Pastor Frank is a graduate of the Moody Bible Institute and alumnus of Midwest Theological Seminary. He has served in various capacities over the years. He has Pastored several churches vocationally in Illinois since 2016, and he also served as a Missionary/Church Planter for the North American Mission Board. Additionally, he served as Leadership Development Team Leader for a church association and has a passion for the Gospel and seeing people grow in their faith.

He is married with three children and loves anything having to do with family.

Samuel Gervasi - Samuel was raised in a Christian home and accepted the Lord at a young age. After sensing God's leading from a bible tract and was baptized.

While attending a Youth Conference answered an altar call to be used by God in a greater way and serve him. Samuel felt God's calling to ministry and answered.

He has served in several capacities in the local church as Worship Leader, Adult Discipleship, Teen Ministry, & Administration. He is an Alumnus of the Moody Bible Institute and loves teaching and serving God by advancing the message of Christ.

MIDWEST CHRISTIAN PUBLISHING